Warrior Attitude

21 Ways to Think & Act like a Warrior That Will Transform Your Outlook on Life

Special **FREE** Bonus Gift for You

To help you achieve more success, there are FREE BONUS RESOURCES for you at:

www.FreeGiftFromAlex.blogspot.com

- Informational Video on Alexander's 3 Keys to Living like a Warrior
- Alexander's Special Free Report

ALEXANDER LANSHE

Copyright © 2014 by Alexander Lanshe

ALL RIGHTS RESERVED. No part of this book or its associated ancillary materials may be reproduced or transmitted in any form or by any means, electronic or mechanical including photocopying, recording, or by any informational storage or retrieval system without permission from the publisher.

PUBLISHED BY: Amazon

DISCLAIMER AND/OR LEGAL NOTICES

While all attempts have been made to verify information provided in this book and its ancillary materials, neither the author nor publisher assumes any responsibility for errors, inaccuracies, or omissions and is not responsible for any financial loss by customer in any manner. Any slights of people or organizations are unintentional. If advice concerning legal, financial, accounting or related matters is needed, the services of a qualified professional should be sought. This book and its associated ancillary materials, including verbal and written training, is not intended for use as a source of legal, financial or accounting advice. You should be aware of the various laws governing business transactions or other business practices in your particular geographical location.

EARNINGS, INCOME & RESULTS DISCLAIMER

With respect to the reliability, accuracy, timeliness, usefulness, adequacy, completeness and/or suitability of information provided in this book, Alexander Lanshe, Alexander Lanshe LLC, its partners, associates, affiliates, consultants, and/or presenters make no warranties, guarantees, representations, or claims of any kind. Readers' results will vary depending on a number of factors. Any and all claims or representations as to income earnings are not to be considered as average earnings. Testimonials are not representative. This book and all products and services are for educational and informational purposes only. Use caution and see the advice of qualified professionals. Check with your accountant, attorney or professional advisor before acting on this or any information. You agree that Alexander Lanshe and/or Alexander Lanshe LLC is not responsible for the success or failure of your personal, business, health or financial decisions relating to any information presented by Alexander Lanshe, Alexander Lanshe LLC, or company products/services. Earnings potential is entirely dependent on the efforts, skills and applications of the individual person.

Any examples, stories, references, or case studies are for illustrative purposes only and should not be interpreted as testimonials and/or examples of what reader and/or consumers can generally expect from the information. No representation in any part of this information, materials and/or seminar training are guarantees or promises for actual performance. Any statements, strategies, concepts, techniques, exercises, and ideas in the information, materials and/or seminar training offered are simply opinion or experience, and thus should not be misinterpreted as promises, typical results or guarantees (expressed or implied). The author and publisher (Alexander Lanshe, Alexander Lanshe LLC (ALLLC) or any of ALLLC's representatives) shall in no way, under any circumstances, be held liable to any party (or third party) for any direct, indirect, punitive, special, incidental or other consequential damages arising directly or indirectly from any use of books, materials and/or seminar trainings, which is provided "as is" and without warranties.

THE IDEAL PROFESSIONAL SPEAKER FOR YOUR NEXT EVENT!

TO CONTACT OR BOOK ALEXANDER TO SPEAK:

Alexander Lanshe, LLC

WarriorSpeaker@gmail.com

www.TheWarriorSpeaker.com

Preface

This book is organized in such a way that every chapter is a stand-alone entity. You need not read in order. Pick whichever chapter catches your eye on any particular day and soak up the fantastic information.

The content of these chapters is based on my 20 years of training with warriors. I have trained with warriors of many diverse backgrounds and experiences ranging from Dignitary Protectors to the Head of the Secret Service.

I trained in martial arts from the time I was 5 until I was 16 years old. I received my black belt in Karate when I was 10. After turning 16 and being awarded my Shodan (1st degree adult black belt), my training shifted to reality based combat. I left the soft matted Dojo and began to learn and train with real-life warriors: Army Rangers, Marine Combat Trainers, Secret Service, Police Officers, Firefighters, and other branches of the military. The principles and attitudes of this book draw largely on my experiences and observations of these great men and women.

I wrote this book with the purpose of sharing my years of experience so that I can contribute to the success of others. We all experience the desire to contribute to the human collective at some point in our lives, and I realized that I had a great storehouse of knowledge from all my training that could positively impact others if I shared it.

I do my best to live by the content of these chapters each and every day of my life and I firmly believe that if you adopt these attitudes and take these actions, you will experience a radical shift in your life as well.

Live in the Battleground,
Alexander Lanshe
Founder of www.TheWarriorSpeaker.com

Table of Contents

- CHAPTER 1: THE ULTIMATE WARRIOR SECRET FOR DESTROYING SADNESS 11
- CHAPTER 2: LIVE IN THE BATTLEGROUND 14
- CHAPTER 3: GIVING CREDIT WHERE CREDIT IS DUE 17
- CHAPTER 4: VICTORY IS RESERVED FOR A CERTAIN TYPE OF PERSON 22
- CHAPTER 5: IT ALL DEPENDS ON WHAT YOU FOCUS ON 25
- CHAPTER 6: ONLY A WARRIOR CAN CHOOSE PACIFISM 30
- CHAPTER 7: IGNORANCE IS FAR FROM BLISS 35
- CHAPTER 8: EVERYTHING YOU DO IS A MATTER OF LIFE AND DEATH 39
- CHAPTER 9: VALOR … A LITTLE USED WORD WITH FORGOTTEN MEANING 44
- CHAPTER 10: WARRIOR FUEL 49
- CHAPTER 11: INCREASE YOUR FEAR 52
- CHAPTER 12: WHY SO FEW ACT IN THE MOMENT OF TRUTH 60
- CHAPTER 13: WHY A SELECT FEW CHOOSE TO MASSACRE THE MANY 63
- CHAPTER 14: "ARE YOU LOOKING FOR A SAFE PLACE?" 68
- CHAPTER 15: MARTIALIZE YOUR LIFE 71

CHAPTER 16: THE MOST ADVANCED PORTABLE SECURITY SYSTEM 74

CHAPTER 17: FRONT TOWARD ENEMY 80

CHAPTER 18: THE MISSING INGREDIENT OF SUCCESS 83

CHAPTER 19: THE THREE INVISIBLE ENEMIES OF LIFE 88

CHAPTER 20: PERPETUAL MOTION 94

CHAPTER 21: NOTHING PERSONAL 97

CHAPTER 1: THE ULTIMATE WARRIOR SECRET FOR DESTROYING SADNESS

"Teachers open the door, but you must enter by yourself" - Chinese Proverb

The Chinese Proverb applies equally well today in the USA as it did back in Ancient China. Teachers can open the door and point the way all day long. Ultimately, the warrior knows that entering through that door is up to them. It is up to you. Have some teachers pointed the way for you and opened a door recently? Take it. Do not stare into the emptiness and say "What am I supposed to do with an open door? Can't you make the doorway move so that I do not have to?" No. The door may move but the doorway will not. You must cross the threshold.

The ultimate warrior secret to destroying sadness is to take action. What kind of action? Almost any action is better than inaction. Take action doing something productive. There is honor to be found in work. Our culture and country has forgotten it. Do not fear work. Fear the lack of work.

It is good to have teachers and coaches open doors and point the way for you. I have many coaches, mentors and am constantly learning. However, learning is not enough. You must apply what you learn. You must do something with it. You must cross the threshold of the doorway and move.

If you are sad, upset, discouraged, or downcast, do not be afraid. This makes you human. You are normal. All of us have fears. All of us are sad from time to time. Warriors take action and combat their sadness and fears. They do not wait for others to fight their battles for them and you shouldn't either.

The great motivational speaker Les Brown once said "There's no point in moaning and groaning about your problems. Half the people you tell don't care and the other half are glad you got 'em." Les was being humorous, but there is a certain degree of truth to his statement. Most people will fall into one of those two categories: uncaring or glad that you are the one with problems.

Warriors don't give other people a chance to fall into those categories, because they take action and crush their sadness. They smother it with action. Their sadness becomes so overwhelmed with action that it has no more room to breathe. Destroy your sadness by taking action. What action? Listen to your intuition. If your gut is telling you that you need to apologize for something to someone, go do it. Right now. If your gut is telling you to begin writing that book you've always wanted to write, start right now. If your gut is saying that you really need to get up off the couch and finish a long-neglected project, do it right now. Take action and crush your sadness beneath it.

CHAPTER 2: LIVE IN THE BATTLEGROUND

There is probably no one in the country who has not heard of the chaos that happened in Ferguson, Missouri. It seemed like every week there was some new tale of violence trending on social media. I confess to knowing little about the case. I know that Officer Wilson is said to have shot and killed Michael Brown. I know that people have reported rioting, looting and all-out chaos erupting over the court decision not to indict Officer Wilson. Regardless of what your opinion of the situation is, there is one angle you have not examined Ferguson from. It is one that warriors have considered and continue to ponder. The importance of living in the battleground.

You may have noticed that I signed the Preface of this book with "Live in the Battleground". Ferguson is a prime example as to why true warriors always live in the battleground. Chaos and violence can erupt at any time. Living in the battleground means that you are aware of this. All grounds are potential battle grounds. Afghanistan is not the only battleground, and employed Soldiers are not always the only combatants on the battlegrounds of life. Ferguson was turned into a real-life battleground with all manner of violence being done by citizen against citizen.

Urban areas are particularly susceptible to this type of chaos. If you live in such an area, take extra precaution to live in the battleground. The mindset is meant to remind the warrior to stay vigilant and to perpetually train and prepare for violence. If you over prepare, and never face violence, you are no worse for the wear. But if you fail to train, fail to prepare and do not mentally live in the battleground, violence is much more likely to devastate you.

Living in the battleground is a mindset warriors adopt in order to always remain aware. Awareness is the warrior's greatest friend and if you consider all grounds to be battlegrounds, you will stay aware. This does not mean you are paranoid. It simply means you watch and observe. You pay attention. You look where and at things others wouldn't look at. You ask good questions and face reality by admitting your vulnerability. Living in the battleground promotes the actions of a vigilant warrior.

Ferguson is one of the ways violence can rear its ugly head. Mass rioting and looting. Vandalism and arson. Those who were prepared and who had the mindset of a warrior largely survived unscathed. Some of those who were not prepared or those who were unaware have suffered at the hands of attackers. Which would you rather be? The prepared warrior, or the unprepared victim? Either way, you live *ON* the battleground each day, the real question is, do you live *IN* it?

Live in the battleground warriors.

CHAPTER 3: GIVING CREDIT WHERE CREDIT IS DUE

A mark of a true warrior is giving credit where credit is due. Warriors recognize the efforts of all. Warriors realize that it is "the little people" that really matter. What is a General without his soldiers? What is a corporate CEO without his team of VP's, accountants, lawyers, salespeople, marketers, and tech department? What is a famous film actress without directors, set-designers, make-up artists, costume designers, script writers, and tech people?

Imagine our film actress. She is beautiful, she is famous and she is amazing at her craft. Now imagine that suddenly, all the directors, set-designers, make-up artists, costume designers, script writers, and film tech people disappeared from the planet. How effective will she be without these people? Sure she can still act, but won't her finished product be lacking? She knows nothing about directing, cannot make her own costumes, and doesn't know a thing about writing dialogue. She can't run the sound board and she surely cannot build a set by herself. How awesome of a movie would that be if it had she in it but lacked all those other people? It wouldn't be very good.

Now imagine a General but all his troops suddenly disappear. How is he to fight the war by himself? The general without his troops is nothing. The CEO now finds himself in the same predicament. All his departments have suddenly vanished. No more lawyers, accountants, salespeople or tech people. How is the CEO to continue running this corporation? Sure he could do everything himself, but how effectively? He likes selling but he has never been any good at legal jargon, accounting, or particularly savvy with technology. The company is doomed in this position. The CEO is nothing without his team. Warriors realize this. A warrior knows that he/she is only as strong as the weakest link in the chain. This is why warriors seek to improve all those around them. They seek to improve all those on their team but most importantly, they give credit where credit is due.

Many times, people will single out one individual and give him or her all the praise for a particular achievement. Be it in show business, Corporate America, or on the battlefield. The egotist is the one who soaks up the glory and says "Thank you, thank you." The warrior is the one who says "Well, first and foremost, I only go as far as my team. Without them, we never could achieved this monumental film, started this tremendous company or won this hard-fought battle."

In an upcoming chapter, I write about Kyle Carpenter, a marine who won the Medal of Honor after he threw his body on top of a live grenade to save his fellow marine. He lost his left eye, needed massive reconstructive surgery on his face, and his left arm is still badly damaged from the 30 bone fractures that occurred when the grenade detonated. After winning the Medal of Honor, he appeared on the David Letterman show. Letterman asked him whether he threw himself on the grenade because that's who Kyle Carpenter is and was before joining the marines or was he just a product of his training? Kyle was given the chance before millions of people to say "Oh yeah, that's me. That's how I've always been. Kyle, the selfless hero." But he didn't. Taking a big sigh before speaking, Kyle said: "I would like to say it was me, but it was my training. The marine core instills in you the proud history we have of other marines who have been heroic and that when you are out in dangerous parts of the world, the marine to your right and left is all you have." He elaborated saying that "We are taught and trained to always look out for our junior marines and that sense of protection is instilled in us from day one." He gave credit to his training. Thereby giving credit to his trainers, and his fellow marines who helped him train. Even after winning the Medal of Honor, the highest military honor we have, he still gave credit to his comrades; to his team.

Be a warrior and give credit where credit is due. Do not glory in yourself and what you have done. Give thanks to all those on your personal team who have supported you and propped you up. "No man is an island" as the saying goes, and I know that I am no different. I thank all of my family, friends, mentors and most importantly I thank God

Almighty for His many blessings. Without God, and without my family, friends, and mentors, I am nothing.

Live in the battleground warriors.

CHAPTER 4: VICTORY IS RESERVED FOR A CERTAIN TYPE OF PERSON

Are you the type of person who is willing to sacrifice and pay the price for what you want or are you the type of person who wants to get something for free? There is a perverted attitude in our culture which seeks to get without giving. To reap without sowing. Victory isn't so easily gained and it cannot be fooled. Lasting victory in life will go to those who have perseverance; to those who pay the price. Which type of person are you?

If you are the type of person who seeks to gain first without giving, you must correct your attitude and approach now. This attitude is most likely the cause of why you cannot win; of why victory eludes you. Again, you cannot trick victory. It comes to those who do what is necessary to obtain it. Thinking otherwise is like expecting to reap a bountiful harvest of corn in the fall when you failed to plant in the spring. If you do not sow, you will not reap. If you do not prepare for victory, you will not be victorious.

The warrior who fails to pay the price of training and preparing for war will likely be the first to die on the battlefield. This applies to life in general; to your life. Victory in marriage goes to those who are intentional about being victorious in their marriage. Victory in business comes to those who are intentional about being victorious in their business. Victory only comes to those who are willing to pay the price.

In our culture, there are many people who believe they should be victorious without having to pay the price. These people miss the entire point. By paying the price, you become someone worthy of victory. The victory is often less important than the person you have to become in order to obtain victory. If you are handed victory without having to pay the price, your perseverance muscle never gets developed. This is why these victories are not sustainable. Because this individual lacks the personal perseverance to forge ahead when things go bad. Many times they often lack a true support system around them. This is because being victorious without paying the price often results in that person becoming a taker, not a giver. They become entitled, since victory was handed to them, and as a result, they become selfish, unattractive people.

Do not attempt to cheat by gaining victory without paying the price. Pay the price. Your character will be strengthened and your perseverance muscle will gain invaluable experience and exercise.

What areas of life do you wish to be victorious in? Answer that question for yourself. Once you have done that, seek out what price you will have to pay to get there. The rest is simply in the doing of the thing. Pay the price. You can either win or lose at life and guess what? The result is up to you.

CHAPTER 5: IT ALL DEPENDS ON WHAT YOU FOCUS ON

There is one mindset shift that most people never think of which can drastically improve all areas of your life. It can improve your relationships, your occupation and your studies in school. It is a simple, yet profound mindset shift that is used by warriors and highly successful individuals. This simple shift is just this: look at all things initially through the lens of similarity rather than dissimilarity.

What does this mean? It means that at first, look at how things are similar. Any things you are contrasting or comparing. Don't let your first question be "How are these things different?" Let your first question be "How are these things similar?"

Example: All human relationships have certain basic characteristics. Your relationship with your mother, father, son, daughter, co-worker, etc. are all different yes, but what characteristic(s) do all those relationships have in common? Trust. You will not have an effective relationship with anyone if you do not trust them and they do not trust you. Fundamentally then, when you are seeking out new relationships, don't focus on how this person is different from you, your spouse or your current friends; look at what is similar. You must build up trust so studying how to build trust and how to be a trustworthy person would be a beneficial thing to study.

The public education system does a fantastic job at making everything have its own box and container. History is separate from math which is separate from chemistry which is separate from dance. Why? Focus first on what makes these things all similar instead of different. Many people bemoan the fact that they don't retain much of what they are taught in school. This problem could be largely remedied if students were taught how all the subjects link together rather than making them all different. As it stands now, if I am a history buff and am taking my math class, I am not shown how math and history go together. I am simply forced to do the same thing everyone is doing. The same goes the opposite direction. The math "nerd" is forced to take in history the same as everyone else. Why? Much greater success could be attained if we said to the history buff student "Tommy, you are going to write a paper on the history of mathematics. Who were the founders of Calculus, Geometry, and Algebra? When did these discoveries occur and what impacts did they have on the world when they happened?" He would research and learn the history of people like Sir Isaac Newton, Archimedes, and Euclid. This would be focusing on the similarities between math and history. Reverse this for the math junkie. Have him crunch the real numbers behind Archimedes' theory of displacement and have him do experiments with Newton's Laws. This way, both students learn. How much do you think they will retain? What will their attitude toward education be? And why? Because they focused on how the subjects go together (are similar) instead of being told "Math goes in this box and history goes in that box".

When I say do this for all things I mean all things. Always focus on the similarities first then focus on the differences. This idea was born from combat and war. Would you rather be taught 50 different ways to use 50 different weapons (sword, spear, bow, arrow, knife, staff, gun, rifle, bayonet, cord, bomb, etc.) or 1 way to use all 50 weapons? Do you think it would be easier to "remember" how to fight using the 50 different ways or remembering only 1 way?

Warriors always focus on the similarities first. What do all humans have in common? Any attacker will have a head. Destruction of this target ensures your survival. Focusing on how to destroy an opponent's head is a common element of all human violence. From this then, learning how to protect your own head becomes very important since you just learned it is every attacker's primary objective. But the point is, why can it be EVERY attacker's primary target? Because anyone who is attacking you is going to have a head. So don't focus on how this opponent is different from that opponent; what do they all have in common? One thing for sure, they all have a head.

If you apply this to everything in your life, you will be radically transformed. It will simplify and defrag your life.

Focus on the similarities, not the differences (at first). There is a time and place for differences, but it is not the first thing. If you always seem to have poor romantic relationships, focus on the similarities of all those relationships. In the similarities you will find the most valuable lessons to be gleaned.

Live like a warrior by focusing on the similarities.

CHAPTER 6: ONLY A WARRIOR CAN CHOOSE PACIFISM

In life, are you the kind of person who values being able to make choices and having many available options or are you the kind of person who enjoys being condemned to act a certain way or to be a certain thing? I value choices. I like having options. When it comes to violence, a warrior is the only one who has choices. As a warrior, I can choose pacifism and I can refuse to fight. Conversely, should things go wrong, I have another option; I can fight. Only warriors are true pacifists because they can do the very thing that ensures that pacifism will win the day; they can be violent.

A non-warrior pacifist has no choices. They have no options. They are pacifists because they must be. They have not the skills nor the heart nor the mind for fighting. Therefore, their stance carries no real nobility. Do we call a person noble who acts out of compulsion? Let me put it another way: If the only thing you could do when someone asked for help was to give help, would you be noble? If I came up to you and said "I need help jumping my car" and you were magically compelled to help anyone who asked for it, would you be noble? No. You aren't helping me because you chose to, you are helping me because you are forced to. Nobility can exist only where there is freedom to choose it's opposite; ignobility. Therefore, when a warrior chooses pacifism or ends a fight before it begins, he/she has done a noble thing. Because the warrior could have done otherwise. He/she could have chosen to hurt, maim or kill the other person. But they chose not to. They chose pacifism. Non-warriors can only be pacifists. They don't choose it for its nobility, they choose it because they have no other choice. If the person they are debating suddenly attacks them shouting "I don't care about your pacifist principles. I'm going to kill you!" The pacifist is in serious trouble unless a warrior comes by to help them. If someone were to do the same to a pacifistic warrior, the warrior can choose option B; to fight. In other words, if diplomacy fails, the warrior can engage in combat. For pacifists, if diplomacy fails, and a fight ensues, they are quick to look around for someone who isn't a pacifist to lend them aid.

If you choose the warrior path, you will then have two options: To be a pacifist or a fighter depending on what the situation dictates. If you choose pacifism without being a warrior, then you are condemned to that path alone and can make no other choice regardless of the circumstances or situation.

Which path you choose is up to you. Again, if you value freedom, choices and options, you would be wise to choose the warrior path. If you don't value having freedom, choices and options, then you may just choose the path of pacifism. Choose wisely. I'll leave you with a hypothetical scenario and I'll let you decide which person you'd rather be in this scenario, the warrior, or the pacifist:

You are sitting on your favorite sofa watching your favorite TV show in your home. It has been a long day at work and you are glad you get to sit down and finally relax a little. Suddenly, a brick comes smashing through your living room window. You see three men in masks storming through the broken window and you hear one of them say "You two handle him (pointing at you) and I'll go find the little girl (meaning your daughter)". You misplaced your cell phone so you are unable to call for help and the two men will be upon you within seconds. The one is already angling off in the direction of the bedrooms where your daughter lies sleeping. You can see it in the eyes of your soon-to-be attackers that they intend to do you great harm, and maybe even kill you. You shudder to think about what they will do to your daughter and how they know that you have a daughter in the first place. What would you rather do? Begin a lecture about the immorality of violence and their actions? Or fight them off until you and your daughter are safe and the attackers are arrested? Could you live with yourself if they beat you nearly to death and kidnapped your daughter or son? The sad part is that you may not have to because they might kill you and then kidnap your daughter. In this moment, which person would you rather be? The warrior or the pacifist? Always remember this quote:

"Only a warrior can choose pacifism, all others are condemned to it." – Unknown

Live in the battleground warriors.

CHAPTER 7: IGNORANCE IS FAR FROM BLISS

There is one threat that is paramount above all others. Greater than any terrorist group, street fighter, or gang of thugs. More efficient than a 1911 pistol and more devastating than an atomic bomb. It injures and kills more people per year than all the weapons and acts of violence from around the world combined. Worst of all, this threat is more subtle and insidious than a deadly virus and will ravage you three times as quickly. This threat is lack of awareness. Awareness? Yes. Lack of awareness kills more people than any other cause or causes combined. Many people could have prevented violence, prepared for it, or combated it had they only been more aware. More people could stave off financial ruin if they were simply more aware of their financial state. More people could overcome addictions and vices if they were simply aware of them in the first place. No problem is treatable or curable without their first being aware of that problem. No market need can be fulfilled if no one is aware of the need. No issue can be resolved without you first being aware of it.

"He who masters others is mighty, he who masters himself is mightier still." - Lao Tzu

The ancient philosopher Lao Tzu spoke true words. To master oneself, you must be aware of yourself. In our age of technology, consumerism, and insane speed, it is easy to forget to study yourself and to become more aware of yourself. Why do you do what you do? Why do you choose to associate with the people you choose to associate with? Why do you work at the place you choose to work? Those are deep questions. A warrior strives to know the whys behind his/her life because the whys are what will compel you when things get tough; and all warriors know that times will get tough. That's a pretty negative outlook, some will say. Okay: I'm positive, things are going to get tough. It is a fact. Lack of awareness makes those tough times even tougher. It needn't be so.

In order to master yourself, you must be aware of yourself. If you are aware of yourself you will also then consider how what you do affects other people (in turn, making you more aware of others). It is not possible to be 100% aware of everything, but the warrior seeks to be as aware as possible. Ignorance is not bliss. At best, ignorance makes one look foolish. At worst, ignorance gets you or other people killed. Warriors do not settle for lack of awareness. They push themselves to become more aware of everything in their world. If you fail to do this, lack of awareness will cause you misery and grief. Many people realize that things are not going their way but they never stop to become aware of why that is or how they can change the situation. Do not settle for lack of awareness. Become aware. Start paying attention to the why's of your life. Start thinking about how and why you do what you do in regards to others and yourself.

To combat violence, be aware of your surroundings in a 360 degree fashion. Take in everyone's emotions, body language, smells, sights, sounds, and textures. Start to feel again. Wake yourself up from the technological trance and begin to feel yourself and the world again. Do not let the number one threat, lack of awareness, be the reason why you failed. Become aware of your problems and what you must do to overcome them and then march proudly forward to do battle.

CHAPTER 8: EVERYTHING YOU DO IS A MATTER OF LIFE AND DEATH

Everything you do is a matter of life and death. How many things? Everything. All things are a matter of life and death. A warrior knows this. The non-warrior does not. It is important to note that all things are a matter of life and death regardless of whether or not you are aware of this fact. Truth is unaffected by anyone's level of awareness or perception. Truth simply is.

C'mon, really? ALL things are a matter of life and death? I can hear you thinking that thought right now. Yes they are. They are because the warrior treats all things as the last time they will do, see, and experience that thing. A warrior has faced the reality that death can come at any moment. This motivates them to treat things with much greater deference, live with much more honor, and to enjoy the many blessings of life.

I want you to imagine with me that you are living in 13th century, feudal Japan. You are a young 20-something who is a Samurai and you are a retainer of a great feudal lord (daimyo). One day, you suddenly receive word from an official messenger that your lord needs your services in combat and you are to make haste to leave immediately. You must go and fight for your lord. How do you think you will say your goodbyes to your family that day compared to other days? How much do you think you will value putting on your armor? How much do you think you will value that last glance of your home?

The warrior does his/her best to treat every moment just like this. As if they had been called off to battle; the battle that will ultimately cost them their life. This level of seriousness does many things to a person who adopts this as a daily attitude. Here are just a few of those things:

1) It makes you appreciate the moment. Since every moment is treated like your last, you appreciate everything to a much greater degree. A beautiful sunset is considered the last one you will see, so you enjoy it more. A kiss with your lover is considered the last kiss you will ever have so

it is enjoyed and treasured immensely.

2) It gives you perspective. Imagine again with me, that you were to die tomorrow. Would you waste your last 24 hours, 1440 minutes, 86,400 seconds on petty drama or quarrels? The warrior does not get caught up in petty drama because they treat each day as their last. Would you really spend your last time on earth with petty family bickering or quarreling with friends?

3) It will change the way you treat people. You will begin to treat people with more kindness and benevolence because each interaction with someone is viewed as your final interaction. This applies especially to people we are close to (family and friends). You tend to take the people closest to you for granted and the warrior remedies this by believing that each interaction with them will be their last. You will hug longer, kiss softer, speak kinder and show more compassion than if you believe you will always have tomorrow to make your wrongs of today better. The warrior knows they are guaranteed no tomorrows.

4) It will change the way you treat yourself. If you knew you were to die tomorrow, wouldn't you be kinder towards

yourself? Wouldn't you give yourself more credit and extend yourself more grace? I would. I would not spend my last 86,400 seconds berating myself for all the things I failed to do or all the things I did wrong. If I knew I was going to die tomorrow, I would spend my time enjoying my last moments with my family and close friends. We would laugh, tell stories of the past, create new moments in the present and say our final goodbyes with passion and love.

Keeping death constantly before your eyes serves to inspire rather than to demotivate. It is the core behind why warriors of the past included things like honor, chivalry, and formalities into their codes of conduct; the presence of death motivated them to live such a life. Knowing they could die at any moment, etiquette was paramount, honor was integral and living a life of passion and vibrant dedication to cause, country, family and self naturally flowed from keeping death ever-present before their minds.

Everything is a matter of life and death because you don't know what moment is your last. Do not live in denial and pretend to be immortal. Time has not lost a battle with any human; it will always win. Instead of denying death, embrace death. Embrace it inasmuch as you are to use death as a motivator to live a life of passion. A life of Warrior hood. Since each day could be your last, treat it as such and watch how your attitude towards life, people and things changes.

Always LIVING in the battleground.

CHAPTER 9: VALOR ... A LITTLE USED WORD WITH FORGOTTEN MEANING

I watched an ESPN special one day titled "Uncommon Valor: the Kyle Carpenter Story". This chapter was inspired by viewing that special. I wanted to share Kyle's incredible story of bravery and courage. The story is quite powerful.

Kyle and a fellow Marine were startled to hear explosions outside their camp; enemy grenades were being thrown at them. Three grenades had already exploded before Kyle and his partner had geared up and made their way outside to combat the enemy. A fourth grenade landed just feet from Kyle and his partner and would explode any second.

'Valor' is defined as "Great courage in the face of danger, especially in battle". What Kyle Carpenter did embodies the definition of valor and is nothing short of extraordinary. Before the grenade could explode, Kyle threw his body on top of it to shield his friend from the explosion. Despite being medically evacuated just minutes after the grenade exploded, Kyle was declared dead upon arrival to the hospital. Doctors would resuscitate Kyle several times and eventually put him in a medically induced coma.

Weeks later, Kyle awoke to Christmas stockings and decorations adorning his hospital room. He looked up and saw his father standing at the end of his bed and spoke his first words in weeks, "Hi Dad." Kyle had lost his right eye, and would eventually need some 40 surgeries to repair his broken body. His right arm sustained over 30 fractures in the explosion. More importantly to Kyle, his partner had survived the grenade attack without injury.

Kyle Carpenter was awarded the Medal of Honor, the highest military honor in existence, for his uncommon valor and bravery in the line of duty. He recently ran a marathon and plans on running in a triathlon next. If ever anyone deserved the title of 'Warrior' it is Kyle Carpenter.

That is the story, now for the commentary after the story. The first thing that went through my mind while I was watching this ESPN special was this: What kind of a person will willingly throw themselves on a live grenade to save their friend? What kind of will, what kind of courage, what kind of pure selflessness is required to do that? And then it hit me: the kind of will, courage and selflessness exhibited by true warriors.

It is staggering to think about. I asked myself "Would you have been able to do what Kyle did?" And I honestly don't know the answer. I would like to think I could have been so selfless but the fact is I don't really know. I have never been placed in a situation where such courage has been required. I do know one thing however; whatever it is that Kyle has that allowed him to make that sacrifice, I want it. If I don't have it yet, I want it.

The filial love Kyle had for his comrade was so powerful that I was overwhelmed with tears while I watched his story and even now as I sit here and type this, my eyes are welling with tears.

I think the lesson that you and I can take away from this story is this: being a warrior is a choice. Kyle had a choice:

to jump on that grenade or to turn away from it and let what would happen, happen. Kyle chose the more difficult yet more heroic act. He chose to sacrifice himself for his friend. In Kyle's mind, this was an act of suicide inasmuch as he was not supposed to survive. He knew full well that he was most likely going to die by throwing himself on that grenade; yet he did it anyway. John 15:13 says "Greater love than this no man hath, that a man lay down his life for his friend." Kyle chose the path of ultimate sacrifice; to die so that his friend could live. Wow.

Make no mistake, Kyle Carpenter is a hero. A true hero. In this culture, we toss around that word 'hero' a great deal. So much so that the meaning has perhaps been dulled due to our desensitization. We say things like "You're my hero" or "X, Y, Z singer/athlete/musician/artist is my hero." Hero is defined as: a person, typically a man, who is admired or idealized for COURAGE, outstanding achievements, or NOBLE qualities. Was Kyle Carpenter courageous? You bet your life he was. Is it noble to give up your life so that your friend can live? As sure as night follows day. Kyle Carpenter is a hero and you and I would be wise to emulate him. To study his life and to figure out how he was able to make such a choice in the face of death. Individuals like Kyle are people worth saying "You are my hero" to. True warriors.

Live with Valor.

CHAPTER 10: WARRIOR FUEL

There is one attribute that is rarely thought about or associated with warriors. It is an extremely powerful attribute and one that if you possess will carry you far in life. It is an attribute that has been given negative connotations over the years and thus has become little discussed. It is perhaps the single most important attribute to possess if you wish to live like a warrior and survive a deadly force encounter. That attribute is defiance.

Defiance is a powerful motivator that can fuel you and cause you to push forward in the face of difficult circumstances. Defiance is not a negative or "bad" quality. It is a positive quality which allows you to say to the world "No. I am not going to be a victim." "Yes, I will stand up for justice, regardless of what you say."

Defiance is what allows great inventors to achieve their dreams. "Electricity? That can't be done." The response of the defiant Nikola Tesla was "Yes it can." "Men can't go to outer space" sounded nice until it was achieved. Some men and women defiantly said "Yes it can and we're going to prove it." "Nobody needs a motor car. You'll never sell these in mass quantities." to which Henry Ford defiantly replied "We'll see."

Defiance for the warrior is what allows them to venture into the heart of violence even when they think they might die. Some, even when they KNOW they will die. How can they do that? Defiance. "You won't survive this mission." "Oh yeah? Watch me." Defiance is a critical attribute to have for anyone who wants to maximize their chances of surviving a violent encounter.

What this means for you is this: Program your mind by telling yourself "I can and will do what is necessary to survive." Do not listen to people who say "this is impossible" or "you can't do that"; be defiant. *Yes, I can survive. Yes, I will survive. Yes, I am willing to do what is necessary to protect myself and my family. I will not cower or give in to society's victim mentality. I am not a victim, I am a survivor.*

Start looking for examples of people who succeeded or survived impossible odds and ask yourself whether or not you see defiance somewhere in the example. Make no mistake, defiance, when appropriately applied, is a very positive trait. It can allow you to survive a deadly attacker; to venture into the heart of darkness when others flee from it. Be defiant. When someone says you cannot survive, be defiant. Yes you can survive. Defiantly stand up for your right to protect yourself.

CHAPTER 11: INCREASE YOUR FEAR

Fear. It is one thing most of try desperately to avoid. I don't mean the fear you experience when watching a scary movie with your friends, or when a sibling jumps out from behind a corner and yells "Boo!" I mean true fear. Fear of not knowing where your next meal is going to come from. The fear of thinking you may have just spent the light bill money on food. The fear of not being sure if you will have any money to live on once you retire. The fear that you will never be able to retire. We try to avoid these fears at all cost. You shouldn't. You need more fear. *What? Is he crazy? Why should I become* MORE *fearful?* Precisely because that which tends to fill fear's void is far more insidious: Denial. Rather than experience and address our fears, we deny that we have them. "No problems here" we say. You have told yourself that lie too many times. You are still telling yourself some of those lies. I know, because I am doing it too. We all do.

Why is denial so insidious? Because it prevents us from taking action. It stops us from fixing the problem because "there is no problem". You need more fear in your life because fear is motivating. True fear goes beyond motivating and becomes sheer compulsion. Here is an example:

In a true story from Gavin de Becker's iconic book, *The Gift of Fear*, he tells of an encounter a client named Kelly described to him. She had been conned into letting a man into her apartment under the pretext of helping her carry groceries she had dropped. Her intuition told her not to let him in but she didn't listen to her intuition. She let him in. He proceeded to rape her. After the ordeal, he closed her bedroom window which had been open and told her, "I'm going to get a drink from the kitchen. You stay here. Once I am done I'll leave, I promise." She responded quietly, "Yes, you know I won't move." Up until that point, she had done everything he asked, so he believed her. What happened next is where Kelly's fear transcended motivation and became pure compulsion. As he was walking out of her room, Kelly rose from the bed, covered in the bed sheets and followed him out. She was so close behind him that he could have felt her breath had she been breathing. She silently followed him as he made his way to the kitchen but once there, she broke off and exited her apartment. She walked straight across the hall to her neighbor's door, opened it, closed the door, motioned to her stunned neighbors to remain silent, and sat on the floor and waited for him to leave. She described to Gavin de Becker how it wasn't her operating her body when she walked out.

"I was observing myself do these things and had no control over my actions. It was a true out of body experience." – Kelly

True fear had compelled her to move; to take action. As it turned out, this particular man had raped and murdered before. He was going to the kitchen for a knife, his murder weapon of choice. Had she stayed on that bed, he would have returned and killed her.

True fear is a motivator and compels you to action. I am not saying I want you to be in Kelly's position. Far from it. But I do want you to face the fears in your life. Why?

Because having a healthy fear of having no money for retirement will motivate you to save money now. Having a healthy fear of not knowing how to protect yourself will motivate you to seek training. Having a healthy fear of not knowing enough to pass your college algebra test will motivate you to study. Denial however will kill you. As surely as the sun rises and falls each day, denial will kill you.

Denial robs you of preparation, it keeps you unaware, and tricks you into thinking "All is well" when all is not well. Think about the examples I listed: Denial will cause you to save zero dollars which will result in bad things when it comes time to retire. Denial will cause you never to train and learn how to protect yourself which will likely result in you being victimized by violence should you be attacked. Denial will cause you not to study for that college algebra test which most likely will result in you failing the exam. Denial is the killer, not fear.

Fear is feedback. If there is something you fear, look at what that fear is trying to tell you. It is trying to save you from future pain. You are tortured by fear of uncertainty of your future when you don't save money because the fear is meant to motivate you to act in ways to assuage that fear (in this case, to save money for retirement and to invest wisely). Taking those actions will alleviate the fear. Denial does not alleviate the fear, it only numbs you to it. It shuts your nerves off, which only serves to mask the symptoms. Chronically, the fear is still there, and the more you attempt to silence your fears with denial, the more painful the outcome will be in the future. The greater the denial, the greater the pain that comes when the thing you deny actually happens.

Denial paralyzes you and renders you incapable of action. The deep sea diver who is fearful of sharks will take the appropriate precautions against them. He also dives knowing that a shark attack is a possibility -- meaning he is at least that much more prepared mentally to face a shark than someone who deep sea dives and has never even considered it a possibility. Which of these two metaphorical divers do you think will panic more when attacked by the Great White Shark? The one who took precautions, prepared, and carried the proper protective tools (shark cage, suit, knives, underwater guns, etc.) or the one who denied that he could ever be attacked by a shark? Who do you think is more likely to survive the encounter?

I will make one more example that applies to more of us than the deep sea diver example: Attacks on our schools. Who do you think is more likely to survive when a mass murderer descends upon the school with the sole mission of racking up a body count? The teachers and students who have mentally and physically prepared for such an event, who are carrying tools to protect themselves and who have taken the necessary preventative measures against such an attacker OR the teachers and students who have denied that such a thing could ever occur? Those who deny that this can and will occur will not prepare. They will not be carrying tools to protect themselves and others and they will oftentimes neglect taking simple preventative measures such as locking their classroom doors.

In this situation, if you fall into the category of denier, it will kill you twice. Once when the bad man murders you. This death is easier. The second and more difficult death is if you survive but watch as dozens of the people around you die. People who you were trusted to protect. You will be mentally slain. Spiritually slain. Your denial never prepared you to deal with the aftermath of a mass slaughtering because you never believed it could happen to you and those you love.

Don't die these deaths. I beseech you not to be this person. Train now. Prepare now. Take the first step and admit that there are bad men in the land who seek to do you harm. Violence is real. Violent people are real. Do not be deceived and seduced by denial. It is an appealing short-term benefit but it is a deadly, long-term poison.

In conclusion, it is okay to be fearful. Let your fears motivate you to become more aware, more alert, more prepared and more active. Use your fears to motivate you to prevent the bad man from ever getting to you and your family. Do not be killed by denial. Do not suppress your fears. Own them. Face them. Allow them to compel you to greater things and to break free from the slavery of denial.

CHAPTER 12: WHY SO FEW ACT IN THE MOMENT OF TRUTH

"If you don't teach people what to do you are teaching them to do nothing." - Lt. Col. Dave Grossman

So few act in the moment of truth simply because they don't know what to do. Indecision paralyzes them. Lack of training manifests as inaction. Most people walk about unarmed; their life-saving tools left at home, their mind dulled and un-sharpened. To survive one must be armed both mentally and physically. Have you trained? Trained for what? To fight when you must. Are you confident that when push comes to shove and you have no other recourse that you could fight for your life and the lives of those you love?

It is my mission and duty to instruct as many as possible in how to protect themselves. By strengthening you I help to strengthen our nation. When you become stronger you help strengthen the nation. Seek out training so that you have the mental and physical abilities to survive a deadly force encounter.

If you are reading this and you are a person who has expertise in personal protection of some form, I implore you to instruct and teach others. Help to strengthen the nation. Help to strengthen your communities. Take your radius of existence and make it a little bit safer. The bad man doesn't wait for us to get training and make our communities more secure. He is a threat now. We must act now. If you fail to teach the people around you, you are teaching them to do nothing. And 'nothing' is not a good response to violence. As any marksman or hunter knows, a stationary target is a dead target.

Warriors attack the attack. We must attack the attack against the enemies of our freedom and safety. Defiantly we must rise up to protect all that we deem most personal. If not you, then who? Ultimately, the only person responsible for your safety is yourself. Take charge of your security today. Whether you are poor or rich, white or black, old or young; it makes no difference. Everyone has the fundamental right to protect themselves. But you must take the initiative. You must take action. There are individuals like myself and many more like me who are determined to equip Americans with the tools they need to protect themselves. Get training. Don't wait until after violence has victimized you. You may not have a 2nd chance. Get the training now.

CHAPTER 13: WHY A SELECT FEW CHOOSE TO MASSACRE THE MANY

Why do some people choose to go into a school seeking to kill as many people as possible? What is the reason behind this? How do we stop them? When and where will the next massacre be? Easy questions to ask but very hard questions to answer. One thing is for certain. There is a cause. There is a thing that causes these murderers to commit these heinous atrocities. What is that thing?

"It's not about what's in their hand, it's about what's in their head." - Lt. Col. Dave Grossman.

Without question, the tool these people hold in their hands is of little consequence. Firearms cannot be the cause. China has experienced several massacres with knives and axes. In December of 2012, a man in China stabbed 23 children and an elderly woman in a primary school. Weapons used in Chinese mass attacks include cleavers, box-cutters, knives and even an axe. The largest single act of mass murder in history took place in Norway. The man killed 69 people and injured 110 more. He impersonated a police officer and was the only man on the island with a gun. Norway's gun laws didn't save them.

A brief browsing of the FBI statistics on weapons used in murders in the US from 2007-2011 include firearms of all sorts. However, I discovered that in each year listed, knives and cutting instruments killed more people than rifles. In fact, rifles and shotguns killed a combined 3918 people from 2007-2011 while knives and cutting instruments killed 8967 people in the same time frame. That's more than double those killed by rifles and shotguns combined.

The point here is this: Human beings will kill with incredible ingenuity. They don't need firearms. If one isn't present, we will make due with something else. 4,055 people were murdered from 2007-2011 with what the FBI calls "Personal Weapons" i.e.: hands, fists, feet, etc. and this doesn't count death by asphyxiation (that was listed as a separate category). The tool is not why people murder. The tool is not the motivation behind a man deciding to kill 69 people at a youth camp in Norway. Nor is a knife the motivation behind why 24 people were stabbed at a

Chinese primary school. The motivation is in the sick heads of the murderers. The common denominator all these incidents have is this: people.

People choose how to use the tools. A firearm used for hunting a deer suddenly becomes a life-giving tool to provide food with. A knife used as a scalpel in an operating room becomes a lifesaving tool. An axe used to chop firewood helps to give you fuel for a fire which gives you heat which can save your life if you are outdoors in the cold. All of these tools do as the person wielding them commands. They have no capacity to do anything of their own accord. They need a master.

Do not be fooled when someone says "Guns kill x number of people per year" or "knives kill x number of people per year" Those tools kill no one. Human beings kill human beings. Period. We desire to focus on the tool because it shields us from the reality that a human being chose to end the life of another person. We don't want to and can't think about that. It scares us too much. However, if we are to protect ourselves and our loved ones, we must face reality.

The reality is that some people choose to kill other people. They willingly take up a tool (knife, gun, axe, poison, etc.) and kill with it. We must admit this if we are to protect ourselves.

Always remember that people kill due to sick minds and souls. The tool is not the cause. The tool carries out the will of its master. A hammer can be used to build a home or crush someone's skull. Whether the hammer is building a house or smashing a skull, it is doing the same thing. It is being swung in the air and made to impact a target. That's it. The only thing that changes is the target. The person has chosen to hit another person instead of hitting the nail. The tool hasn't changed, but the target and the intention of the person wielding it has.

"It's not about what is in their hand, it's about what is in their head." - Lt. Col. Dave Grossman.

CHAPTER 14: "ARE YOU LOOKING FOR A SAFE PLACE?"

I have had the great privilege of listening to Lt. Col. (RET) Dave Grossman speak multiple times at events. The Col. is a former Army Ranger and Psychology Professor at West Point. He uses his specialized knowledge to inform people about the realities of combat, both physically and mentally. But that is not why I am writing today. Today, I want to share a story that he told at the end of his speech that I found very powerful. The following is my paraphrase of the Col's story:

"It was a cold December day during WWII in the Ardennes Forest. The Germans were making a surprise offensive. The ensuing battle of which became known as the Battle of the Bulge. The US troops were getting their tails kicked and the enemy had them on the run. Reinforcements were needed, so the Army Rangers were called in; the 82nd Airborne Division. As it happened, a US tank was fleeing from the German offensive when he saw a lone man standing in the middle of the road. The Sergeant in the tank could tell that this was a US soldier. The soldier had a bazooka slung over his shoulder and his rifle in his hands. He looked stoic, like an immovable marble statue. The man was PFC Martin, 325th Glider Infantry Regiment of the 82nd Airborne Division. The tank rolled to a stop and PFC Martin asked the Sergeant inside the tank "Hey buddy, are you looking for a safe place?" And the Sergeant said "Why yes, yes we are." To which PFC Martin calmly but confidently replied "Then pull your vehicle behind me. I'm the 82nd Airborne, and this is as far as the bastards are going."

To hear Col. Grossman tell this story is to get goose bumps of a profound kind. The US won the Battle of the Bulge. It was a battle that perhaps saved the entire Western world. The courage and conviction showed by PFC Martin is indicative of the Army Rangers but it can also be indicative of you. You can be a PFC Martin for your family friends. When chaos surrounds you and the enemy is advancing, will you cower and be another victim or will you be the one to say to people "Hey buddy, you looking for a safe place?

Then get behind me." Get behind me and be protected. I have resolved to be this person. Have you? Have you trained and prepared to the best of your ability in order to protect those you love? Prepare and train now so that when violence rears its ugly head you can say to those you love "Hey buddy, are you looking for a safe place? Then get behind me. Because I'm a warrior. And this is as far as the bastards are going."

CHAPTER 15: MARTIALIZE YOUR LIFE

'Martial' is a word that is thrown around with little or no thought as to what it means. It is perhaps most familiar in this country when someone says 'Martial Law'. Most of us can visualize what that may look like or entail, but how about the word 'Martial' as a stand-alone word? What images does it conjure? For me, two words spring before my mind when that word is uttered: Seriousness and consequences.

Martial Science is precisely that: a serious study of combat, violence and aggression and the consequences thereof. 'Martial' evokes images of war, of seriousness and of facing extreme consequences. As a warrior, I encourage you to martialize your life. Why? If you live in a martial way you will take life more seriously which will automatically make you more aware of potential consequences of your behavior. For a warrior, every day is a martial day. The days in the Dojo or shooting range are not the only times a warrior is martial. They are martial every day. Serious, aware, alert, and ready to combat the enemy whenever necessary.

This does not mean you must cease having fun, smiling, or being joyful. Just the opposite will happen. The more serious you take life and the more soberly you contemplate how quickly death could descend upon you will cause you to get more joy and value out of each moment. The warriors I have met in my life value their families more than any other people I have met because they soberly contemplate how precious life is. They walk the martial path.

Living a martial life allows you to keep petty things in perspective. It helps motivate you to not waste your time on things and people who don't matter because you realize how short life really is. You value the little things because at the end of the day you realize that they are actually the big things. Living the martial way sobers you up and makes you consciously choose to live an active, vibrant and passionate life. Why? Because death can summon you at any moment. A warrior knows that he/she is not guaranteed another breath and as such they tend to live more consciously, actively and passionately.

I encourage you to martialize your life as soon as possible so that you can take more joy out of each moment. Being a warrior and being martial go hand-in-hand. How can you be martial? Take life seriously. Look at the consequences of your behavior and how it affects others. Raise your level of awareness and take these things into account and you are on your way living life martially.

CHAPTER 16: THE MOST ADVANCED PORTABLE SECURITY SYSTEM

There is a portable security system that you need to invest in right now. It is amazingly simple, affordable, and comes pre-installed. It analyzes thousands of stimuli per second and can make split-second judgments as to whether you are being or are going to be threatened. What if I told you this powerful and portable security system comes as standard issue equipment to all human beings? This means that you currently own it and have used it before. In fact, you use it so frequently that you don't even realize when you are using it. We have a more common name for this portable security system; we call it intuition.

Gavin de Becker, one of the world's foremost experts on violence prediction and threat analysis, talks about how our intuition works every day to keep us safe and secure. In his iconic book, *The Gift of Fear*, Gavin de Becker informs readers just like you that you already have the world's most sophisticated protection device ever created: your intuition.

Using examples from 30+ years in the field of predicting violence and protecting clients, de Becker expounds on how listening to your own intuition can save your life. Following those weird "gut feelings" can often save you from being a victim of violence.

One of the interesting things I learned from studying Mr. de Becker's book (I am in the process of reading it for a 3rd time) is that although we all have this fantastic protection device, many of us silence it when it is sending us signals. No other creature on earth questions the fear signals they receive, but you do. After something happened, have you ever said "I knew I shouldn't have done that"? This shows that you intuitively got a signal to not do that thing but you ignored the signs and did them anyway. Our intuition protects us from many different things besides violence but it is in the presence of true fear that our intuition does its most impressive work.

Women often obey their intuition more than men because intuition has been labeled "feminine." I am here to tell you that intuition is gender neutral. Both of us have it and both of us are capable of using it. The most important thing I gleaned from Mr. de Becker's book is that when you are receiving feelings or vibes from your intuition, do not ignore it. The example he uses goes as follows: (if you are a female reading this, place yourself in this woman's shoes).

Cathy is standing in front of an elevator at work late in the evening; she is one of the last to leave that day. After patiently waiting for the elevator, it opens to reveal one lone occupant; a man. Something about this man is off-putting to Cathy, she cannot quite put her finger on what, but she knows something is. Maybe it is the late hour, maybe it is his disheveled appearance, maybe it is because she simply doesn't want to be alone with someone. Whatever the reason, Cathy begins to chastise herself. "I can't believe you are doing this again," she says to herself. "I am not going to live like this. How can I be rude and let this elevator door slam in this man's face? I have no reason to be apprehensive. Stop being so silly." And after having successfully used logic to pacify her fears, she gets in the elevator with him. Now I ask you, what is sillier? Letting the elevator close in his face to wait for the next elevator or (as Mr. de Becker says in his book) "climbing into a soundproof, steel chamber to be alone with a man she is afraid of"? Have you ever used logic like Cathy did to talk yourself out of following your intuition? I know I have.

To give one more example from the book, a woman (let's call her Joan) took her teenage son to a Physician for a consultation about an ear infection. After being examined it was determined that he needed surgery to correct an inner ear issue. Several weeks later, she brought her son (let's call him Sam) to the hospital for the operation. While she was in the room with Sam and the doctor who would perform the surgery, a loud voice suddenly rang loud and clear in her mind "Cancel the operation." She couldn't understand why she had this feeling or where it was coming from but she could not silence its message "Cancel the operation." She analyzed why she should do such a thing and eventually talked herself into believing that everything was ok. The operation went forward as planned and Sam died during the procedure. It turns out, the doctor who was going to do the surgery had been someone the hospital staff had observed sleeping during previous surgeries (Joan was not aware of this fact). Somehow, Joan's intuition perceived something about the doctor that was so profound it caused it to shout "Cancel the operation" but Joan ignored it.

This is not meant to send you into a state of paranoia but rather to empower you that your intuition is already a finely tuned protection device. You have already been pre-installed with a phenomenal portable security system that works constantly to keep you safe. You use it constantly while driving, making split-second judgments about when this person will merge, stop, swerve, speed up, etc. and you navigate it daily with ease. Listen to this process when it comes to predicting violence; when it comes to protecting yourself. Better to let the elevator close and wait two more minutes for a second elevator than to ignore your intuition, climb into the steel chamber and be attacked.

You have the ability to protect yourself. Training should give you the physical tools to protect yourself which will compliment your intuition. Adding solid physical skills like personal protection, firearm training, blade training, etc. to your already amazing intuition will make you a formidable opponent and will place you in the "I choose not to be a victim" category. I am here to instruct you with the physical skills and warrior mindset necessary to combat violence in your life but your intuition doesn't need my help. It already works and works well. Start listening to it. Warriors know their intuition is there to protect them and they listen to it.

CHAPTER 17: FRONT TOWARD ENEMY

Picture a claymore mine in your mind. Can you see it? This weapon has inscribed on its face, a very powerful three word phrase which is one that is embraced by warriors all over the world. It is a phrase that I have embraced and use it to motivate me when I am faced with challenges. The phrase is simple, yet evokes imagery that is compelling and fueling. The acronym is F-T-E which stands for: Front Toward Enemy.

"Front Toward Enemy" is a quick phrase that can be said when one is feeling down, oppressed, or beaten. Remind yourself to keep your front toward your enemy. Warriors know that many times in battles, you will not feel "up to" fighting. The enemy however does not care that you feel this way. Who is the enemy? It can be an assailant who has broken into your home or it can be that alarm clock sounding off annoyingly at 5am for your workout. Whichever it is, you put your front to your enemy.

The majority of us in this country will never be faced with a serious deadly threat. Your enemy will appear in different forms besides that of a hooded attacker in a dark alley. Your enemy may be the sweet tooth you have that is costing you your health. It may be a challenging In-law you face every time you have a family get-together. It may be your job that you know deep down isn't what you were meant to do but you must do in order to pay the bills and keep food on the table. Whatever it is, you face it. You stand up and boldly face it. Like a warrior you face your enemy in whatever form it appears and you make sure that your enemy knows you will not give in; that there is no surrender in you.

If in fact your enemy is a hooded attacker who means to do you harm, you face that enemy too. You place yourself between them and your family and you face the enemy with a firm look of immovability and resolution. For if you will not act, who will? If you will not face your enemies, who will face them for you? Do not be deceived into believing there will always be a superhero to come "save the day." The truth is, real life superheroes exist in the form of people just like you. Men and women who boldly stand up and face real world enemies and problems; those are the superheroes. You can be one of them, and it all starts with facing your enemy.

I challenge you to step outside your comfort zone and boldly face the enemies in your life. Your alarm clock, your sugar craving, your feelings of inadequacy, your dwindling finances; whatever the enemy may be. Know that you can choose to be a warrior and that you can conquer all those things. And it all starts by placing your front toward your enemy.

CHAPTER 18: THE MISSING INGREDIENT OF SUCCESS

I want to share with you the missing ingredient that if utilized more frequently and appropriately, would facilitate and enable a greater number of people to achieve success than are currently doing so. This ingredient is a simple one, but extremely potent. It is an ancient ingredient and is always utilized by a warrior or a warrior trainer. Too much of this ingredient is fatal, but if this ingredient is not present at all, that is also fatal. Fatal to character, fatal to proper development, and fatal to the proper forging of the warrior spirit which is necessary to survive and carry on through struggles. The name of this ancient ingredient is pain.

Pain in the appropriate and well rationed amounts, is absolutely essential to forging a warrior. Can you imagine training to fight but never fighting? Training to fight but never being hit or impacted in any way? Look at it this way: can a football player properly prepare for the season if he were never to receive and give impact? "Let's just do calisthenics coach. We don't need to actually practice tackling or being tackled." This player would be scorned by the coach. And rightly so. "How do you expect to be ready if you don't ever get tackled or tackle someone son?" Exactly. The football player must feel the impact, feel the pain.

The pain I am referring to is not one of debilitating injury. It is the pain appropriate to one's task. A football player must be tackled and tackle others. A soldier must be hit, feel some pain, in order to simulate combat. Modern day soldiers are often shot with rubber bullets, airsoft BB's and other devices to deliver some pain so that engaging in a shooting conflict is more realistic. Shooting down range is not enough. You must shoot down range while being shot at and feel the impact of dummy rounds beating against you.

Your life is no different. You must feel an appropriate amount of pain in order to facilitate success. If you are too pampered and are never made to struggle (feel the pain) how will you persevere when things get tough? You won't.

You will give up. You will surrender; and life is merciless. If you surrender to life, it will do with you as it will with complete and utter disregard for you, your feelings, your desires and your happiness. A warrior knows this. This is why the warrior trains. This is why the warrior embraces pain. People who train to avoid all pain are missing the point. In a real fight, you will get hit. You will trip and fall (or be thrown down). You will get scraped, you will get bruised. If weapons are involved, you will get hit, cut, shot with them. Therefore, you must be able to experience pain and continue. You must be able to feel pain and persevere because if you surrender, your enemy (and life) are merciless.

Warriors know that sometimes they need to be made uncomfortable. Growth happens just past the point of comfort. Warriors do not like being coddled by others. Why? Because life will not coddle them. The world will not coddle them. Give them appropriate pain now, to avoid disaster in the future. There is a quote that goes: "Pain is the best teacher but nobody wants to be his student." No pain is comfortable at the time. That is precisely the point.

Life will not always be comfortable. Only those who can handle and deal with a little pain will be successful. Your relationships will cause you pain. Your job will cause you pain. Pursuing your dream will cause you pain. Standing up for what you believe in will cause you pain. It is unavoidable. And since the warrior knows that it is impossible to avoid all pain, the warrior trains to endure pain; to be able to follow through and carry on in spite of pain. They refuse to surrender to life and pain. Because here is the real secret: If you surrender, you will still feel pain; except now, the pain will be dealt on life's terms, not yours. If you are going to feel pain, it may as well be on your terms. If you must feel pain, feel pain that will be instructional and serve to help you learn a lesson that you can use to further your dream and arrive at the success you desire.

Embrace pain. Embrace discomfort. Become comfortable with pain. Allow it to teach you lessons. It will teach you many things if you are listening. Live like a warrior and use pain to your advantage as a great teacher and you will be much farther down the path to success than most people.

CHAPTER 19: THE THREE INVISIBLE ENEMIES OF LIFE

In your life, right now, are three invisible enemies. They assail you each and every day, hoping to defeat you. They are not always easy to defeat, because fighting the unseen can be difficult. However, as warriors, we must be ready and willing to do battle with ALL enemies, both seen and unseen. I am going to share with you what those three enemies are and how you can be better prepared and equipped to defeat them.

1) The first (and perhaps most potent) invisible enemy is **IGNORANCE**. Ignorance is an insidious foe because we often are unaware of when it is effecting us. Ignorance limits our ability to achieve, narrows our vision, and is the main ingredient in many self-destructive thoughts such as prejudices, biases, and even vices. Ignorance is crippling because it blinds us to reality and as a warrior, our first task is to know and define reality so that we are able to fight.

Fear not! Ignorance can be defeated. Simply knowing that ignorance is an enemy is a giant leap in that direction. Once ignorance has been identified as an enemy, it becomes fairly easy to combat. Once you realize you have a level of incompetency (i.e.: the level at which you become ignorant) in every area of knowledge, you can begin to become more knowledgeable.

One good habit is to read about at least 1 thing you know nothing about each day. You'll be amazed at how this sparks your thinking and where it can lead. Some sparks ignite massive infernos. Read about things you know nothing about but also dive deeper into your passions each day. Few people know any subject in any great depth. Know your passions with a depth that most do not. Try to discover one new thing about the things (or persons) you love each day and the empty void of ignorance will slowly be filled with knowledge.

2) The second invisible enemy is **CARELESSNESS**. Carelessness can occur in any area of your life from handling a firearm to not being aware of how your words affect those around you. Carelessness almost always results

from a lack of awareness (or ignorance). Carelessness can devastate relationships and cause us great harm. A warrior strives to be ever aware so that carelessness does not occur.

Dismantling ignorance automatically solves many carelessness problems since many instances of carelessness arise precisely due to ignorance. However, you can be intelligent, informed, and yet still careless. One way to avoid being careless is to constantly keep asking yourself "what are the consequences if I do/say x?" Ancient Japanese samurai who trained with razor sharp swords (katana) had to be very careful due to the dire consequences of being careless with a sword. Modern warriors and fighters use that same level of carefulness while using firearms because the consequences of being careless are extremely high. Warriors combat carelessness through the development of good etiquette (postures, rituals, handling of weaponry). When good etiquette is forged as a habit, you are much less likely to be careless. Apply the warrior mindset of treating all "weapons" with respect, to people. Treat all people with respect and make good manners a habit and you will be far less careless.

3) The third and final invisible enemy is **COMPLACENCY**. This enemy particularly affects one group of people; the ones who "know-it-all" already. In the warrior arena, a major cause of firearm "accidents" where people are killed or injured is due to someone who got complacent with a firearm and didn't check to ensure the firearm was unloaded or made safe before doing an activity and then they shot themselves or someone else. In these cases, it was not because this person was ignorant of firearms, nor because they were careless. They got complacent. "I already know this" was their attitude and it resulted in them not doing their due diligence which led to an injury or death.

In your own life, complacency can show up everywhere. "I already worked hard on my relationship with my girlfriend/spouse so I don't need to work hard anymore." This is a sabotaging thought which can lead to relationship ruin. You must always work to overcome the 2nd Law of Thermodynamics: any place/thing/relationship left to itself will decay and break down. Yes, the Law of Entropy applies to your relationships. Battle complacency by having good habits (again, good manners) guide you. Do not deviate from them. With firearms, I ALWAYS check and double check that the firearm is clear of any ammunition before putting it away. I trust NO ONE when they say "It's ok, it's unloaded." Not good enough; I check. "But I just unloaded it 2 seconds ago." I don't care. I am checking it. That process is never compromised in order to ensure that I do not get complacent. Keep the consequences of being complacent in mind and you will be far less likely to get complacent. Do you want your spouse to leave you because you stopped working on the relationship? Complacency is an absolute relationship killer and it will destroy all the relationships you have unless you fight it tenaciously like a warrior. Fight it with good etiquette, remembering consequences always, and treating life with the seriousness that it deserves.

CHAPTER 20: PERPETUAL MOTION

I believe that the first task of a leader and a warrior to is to define reality. How can a warrior combat life's enemies and problems if that warrior is not operating in reality? My task and mission is to share with you what you NEED to hear, not what you WANT to hear so that you can protect yourself, your family, your friends and achieve as much success as possible.

Success (especially in the US) is currently portrayed as an actual thing you can achieve; something substantive you can hold, see and touch. It is a final destination, a place you "get to". I reject that notion. The truth about success is this: Unless you continually put forth effort to grow, you will be left behind.

Once you "arrive" at success, you must continually grow and strive to keep moving forward or else the riptide of life will sweep you out to sea and drown you. I don't really like calling success a destination because that implies that once you get there that you can cease putting forth effort; you can rest. I think it fools people into thinking that succeeding is easier than it is. Succeeding is hard. Why? Because it takes continual effort. The truth is, there is no rest if you want to be successful. Life is motion and death is the cessation of motion. Think about it. Why do you really die? And when does it happen? You die when all the cells in your body cease moving. A flat-line means your heart has STOPPED beating. It was beating a moment before, but now it beats no more.

What's the lesson? Don't stop moving. As a shark must continually swim or die, so you must do. We are all really like sharks: motion will keep us alive, non-motion will kill us. The ugly truth about success is that there is no destination, there is no "place" you can arrive at. It is an ocean with no islands, no shores; just an eternal ocean. This is daunting, and it is why so many sink. In order to succeed you must swim forever; no rest. It is a never-ending journey of motion until you die. All the most successful people I have ever been around, seen or have the privilege to know and call friends are those who keep moving. I have a mentor who is a billionaire entrepreneur and he keeps moving forward. He never stops. No rest. Another mentor is the leading authority on martial sciences and personal protection and he is ALWAYS training.

Do not fall for the myth that you can arrive at success. It is a phantom you will chase and never catch; or worse still, you will "catch" it and then you will unknowingly be swept away in the riptide and drown thinking that you "caught" success. Once you cease swimming you will begin to lose; you will slowly begin to drown. Soldiers and warriors on the combat field will tell you the same thing: keep moving. If you are a stationary target, you will die. Move. Move and succeed.

CHAPTER 21: NOTHING PERSONAL

A commander on a battlefield takes in lots of information. The survival of your troops depends on your ability to make the best judgments and lead them in the right course of action. This can only be done if you remain as impartial as possible, take in all the information and make the best choice based on that information.

As a commander, many soldiers will be communicating with you about what you should do, or how they feel about this or that course of action. Those troops may not like the commander's choice, and that could hurt the commander if he/she takes that personally. The commander must remain impartial and make the best choice, but most importantly, listen to ALL THE INFORMATION and not discount something because it is uncomfortable. The same goes for your relationship.

Your spouse or significant other will often times present you with a piece of information. It could be that their feelings were hurt by something you said to them. In these moments, take a deep breath, and really listen to what your spouse/partner is saying. Very often, they are not attacking you, but instead are unhappy with a behavior or a thing that you did or said. A good commander can divorce themselves from the things they said or did in a given moment. If you do the same, your relationships will be far more rewarding in the form of deeper and more meaningful communication. Realize that your partner is upset with the behavior or words spoken and not upset with you. They simply would like the behavior to change. Remain impartial and don't take things personally. Be like the good commander.

A good rule of thumb is to always assume that what someone is saying to you is not personal unless they specifically declare it to be so. Listen to what they are saying. Usually it is something like "I don't like when you do this," or "I don't like when you say that," not that they don't like you. We tend to hear the word 'you' and tune the rest out. Don't. Listen to the whole thing and realize they often simply want a behavior corrected or a misspoken word apologized for. Don't take it personally. Remain impartial. Assume they still love you but are upset with the action or word and it often times may turn out to be just that. Keep taking things personally and assume they don't love you, and it may quickly become exactly as you predict. Don't engage in this self-fulfilling prophecy. Remain impartial and listen to all the available information just as a good commander would.

Living in the Battleground.

Have any warrior stories of your own that you would like to share? Overcome any adversity that you would like to share? Send me an email at

WarriorSpeaker@gmail.com

Also, don't forget to redeem your FREE gifts at:

www.FreeGiftFromAlex.blogspot.com

- Informational Video on Living like a Warrior

- Special Warrior Speaker Free Report

If you want to join my growing Warrior Community, check out my social media pages:

- www.facebook.com/warriorspeaker
- www.twitter.com/WarriorSpeaker

Printed in Great Britain
by Amazon.co.uk, Ltd.,
Marston Gate.